VASCO DA GAMA

First European to Reach India by Sea

JENNIFER LANDAU

Published in 2017 by The Rosen Publishing Group, Inc.
29 East 21st Street, New York, NY 10010

Library of Congress Cataloging-in-Publication Data

Names: Landau, Jennifer, 1961- author.
Title: Vasco da Gama : first European to reach India by sea / Jennifer Landau.
Description: First edition. | New York: Rosen Publishing, 2017. | Series: Spotlight on explorers and colonization | Includes bibliographical references and index. | Audience: Grade 5 to 10.
Identifiers: LCCN 2015048844 | ISBN 9781477788271 (library bound) | ISBN 9781477788257 (pbk.) | ISBN 9781477788264 (6-pack)
Subjects: LCSH: Gama, Vasco da, 1469-1524--Juvenile literature. | Explorers--Portugal--Biography--Juvenile literature. | India--Discovery and exploration--Portuguese--Juvenile literature. | Discoveries in geography--Portuguese--Juvenile literature.
Classification: LCC G286.G2 L36 2016 | DDC 910.92--dc23
LC record available at http://lccn.loc.gov/2015048844

Manufactured in the United States of America

CONTENTS

SEARCHING FOR A NEW ROUTE

Portuguese explorer Vasco da Gama was a brave, bold, and at times brutal adventurer. In 1498, da Gama was the first European to find an all-sea route to India. During the 1400s, Portugal wanted to travel by sea in order to bypass the Arab traders who controlled the land route to central Asia. This land route, known as the Silk Road after the silk that traders in China sold, connected Europe to Asia. The Silk Road opened trade and communication between different cultures, but the route was long and dangerous.

If the Portuguese traveled by sea, they could get the gold, silk, and spices

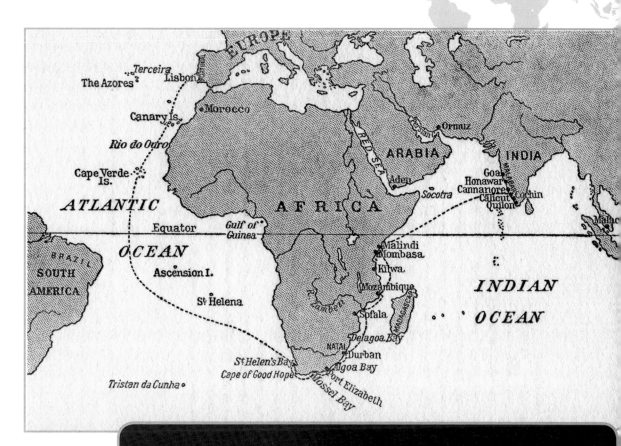

The dotted line on this map shows the route of Vasco da Gama's first voyage from Lisbon, Portugal, to Calicut, India.

Europeans wanted directly from India at a much lower price. While they traveled, da Gama and his men, who were Christians, hoped to convert the Muslims they met to Christianity. The sailors were also looking for a mythical Christian king named Prester John, who many believed lived in Africa, although he was never found.

THE AGE OF DISCOVERY

In the mid-to-late 1300s, nearly one-third of Europe's population died from a bacterial illness called the bubonic plague. Although this disease killed millions, the survivors had more food and more room to move about, which made for a healthier population.

In the 1400s, advances in navigation and shipbuilding, combined with a desire to trade and to spread the Christian religion, led to the Age of Discovery. Leading this movement was Portugal's Prince Henry the Navigator, son of King John I. From 1419 until his death in 1460, Prince Henry sent sea expeditions down the west coast of Africa. These expeditions furthered

l'Infant Don henri.

Portugal's knowledge of foreign lands. On these voyages, explorers acquired gold and ivory and prisoners, who were sold as slaves.

After Henry's death, these expeditions continued. In 1488, Bartolomeu Dias sailed around the southern tip of Africa, which was the farthest any European had sailed up to that point.

EARLY LIFE OF AN EXPLORER

There is uncertainty surrounding Vasco da Gama's boyhood, since few records were kept at the time. Historians believe that he was born in 1469 in the small port city of Sines, Portugal. His father, Estevao, was a knight in service to Ferdinand, the Duke of Viseu, who was Henry the Navigator's heir.

As the son of a nobleman, da Gama was likely sent away to school in the city of Évora to study subjects such as astronomy, navigation, and math. Évora was later one of the sites of the Portuguese Inquisition, in which the Catholic Church harassed or killed Muslims and Jews who refused to convert to Catholicism.

In 1492, King John II asked da Gama to capture all the French ships in Portuguese harbors and take their goods. This action was to get back at the French for seizing a Portuguese ship on its way home from Africa and stealing all of the gold on board. Da Gama was successful in his mission. His victory earned him a reputation as a daring and forceful leader.

HEADING OUT TO SEA

Portugal's King Manuel I chose da Gama to lead the 1497 expedition to India. The captain-major, as da Gama was called, had 170 men and four ships in his charge: the *São Gabriel,* the *São Rafael,* the *Berrio*, and a store ship to hold supplies.

The fleet headed out from the capital city of Lisbon on July 8, 1497. Later that month, da Gama and his crew stopped at the Cape Verde Islands to get more supplies.

Da Gama then ordered his men to head away from the African coast. The captain-major was hoping to avoid the storms and

This sixteenth-century pen-and-ink drawing shows the four ships used in Vasco da Gama's first voyage to India.

winds that had thrown other explorers off course. Months went by as they sailed the Atlantic, but finally the ships reached a bay that da Gama named St. Helena Bay. The sailors had traveled more than 3,000 miles (4,828 kilometers). Much of what is known about da Gama's voyage is from a journal called the *Roteiro,* which was kept by an unknown crewmember.

MAKING A VOW

Once settled near the shore at St. Helena Bay, da Gama's crew began cleaning the ships, which had become filthy with barnacles, worms, and debris. Some of da Gama's men went ashore to find fresh water and wood. They met the local people, and at first the two groups got along. The Portuguese exchanged coins for conch shells and fans and gave the Africans bells and tin rings.

A sailor named Fernao Velloso went off with the Africans to learn more about their culture. There was an argument between Velloso and his hosts, and the Africans chased him down to the beach. As Velloso's shipmates came to rescue him, Velloso was attacked with spears, stones, and arrows.

Da Gama and his men stopped at St. Helena Bay, shown here in the present day, to clean their ships and get fresh supplies.

After da Gama was struck in the thigh, he ordered his men to shoot arrows at the Africans. Da Gama vowed to never again let his guard down with those he met on his journey. This vow would have serious consequences as time went on.

ROUNDING THE CAPE

Da Gama's first attempts to round the Cape of Good Hope were made difficult by fierce south-southwest winds. Finally, on November 22, 1497, the fleet was successful in going around the cape. The ships sailed toward Mossel Bay in what is now South Africa. The first contact with the Africans who lived there went well. In time, however, the Africans grew angry that the Portuguese were taking all of their water. The sailors returned to their ships, but they set off cannon fire to prove that they could fight the Africans if needed.

Thirteen days in, the fleet left Mossel Bay and headed up the east coast of Africa. By

After da Gama's fleet rounded the Cape of Good Hope in November of 1497, they headed toward Mossel Bay, in what is now South Africa.

this time, many crewmembers were sick with scurvy. Vasco da Gama's brother Paulo, who was the captain of the *São Rafael*, tended to the sick men. He even gave some of his own supply of medicine to the sailors. Sadly, many still died of this frightening disease.

TENSION IN MOZAMBIQUE

In early 1498, da Gama and his men anchored their ships in Mozambique, on the southeast coast of Africa. The Africans in Mozambique were Muslims. The Portuguese and Africans were wary of each other, as Muslims and Christians had clashed over territory and religion for many years. Da Gama met with the local sultan, who was insulted by the cheap gifts that da Gama offered. The sultan did agree to give da Gama two maritime pilots to help steer the ships through the Indian Ocean.

Tensions grew when one of the pilots left the ship. The Portuguese fired guns at the Muslims, who were armed with bows and arrows. The Portuguese left, but when they

This statue of Vasco da Gama stands outside the chapel and palace of São Paulo in Mozambique, on the southeast coast of Africa.

came back in search of drinking water, they were confronted by another group of Africans. Da Gama had his men strike the town with gunfire and bombards. The Africans ran away, and da Gama took the water his sailors needed.

MOMBASA AND MALINDI

Da Gama's fleet reached the port city of Mombasa, in what is now Kenya, in April 1498. Da Gama was given a tour and was told there were Christians in Mombasa. The captain-major feared that he was being set up for an attack in retaliation for his attack on the people of Mozambique. He tortured two men he had captured in Mozambique, and they admitted a plan was in place to get back at the Portuguese. When the Africans swam up to the ships carrying knives, a battle broke out. In the end, the Portuguese won the battle.

The fleet headed to Malindi, where they were treated well by the local sultan. He sent

PEPTONE DE VIANDE DE LA COMPAGNIE LIEBIG.

La Découverte de la route des Indes.
3. Entrevue de Vasco de Gama (et de son frère Paul) avec
le souverain de Mélinde (côte de Zanguebar). Mai 1498.

In this picture, da Gama and his brother Paulo are shown meeting with the sultan of Malindi in May of 1498.

gifts of spices out to da Gama's ships. When the two men met, the sultan agreed to send letters of greeting to King Manuel I to show that da Gama had reached the shores of Malindi. Da Gama's stay in Malindi brought him much cheer.

A DREAM FULFILLED

It took the Portuguese sailors over twenty days to reach a kingdom called Calicut on India's southwestern coast. They had fulfilled their dream of sailing to India, making them the first Europeans to do so.

Calicut was the busiest port in India and had been the center of the international spice trade for hundreds of years. Traders from such places as Persia, Egypt, and Arabia came to Calicut to do business.

There were people of different religions in Calicut, but the Muslims were in charge of much of the trade. The Muslims got along with the leader of Calicut, although he was of the Hindu faith. The leader was known as the Samutiri, which means "ruler" in the

This sixteenth-century Flemish tapestry shows da Gama arriving in Calicut, India, after a long and dangerous journey. He was the first European to find an all-sea route to India.

Malayalam language. The Portuguese called him the Zamorin. The Muslims valued their relationship with the Zamorin and did not want to give up control of the local trade to the visiting Christians.

MEETING THE ZAMORIN

On May 28, 1498, da Gama met the Zamorin and introduced himself as an ambassador for the king of Portugal. The following day, da Gama showed the Zamorin's assistants the gifts he had brought their ruler, including striped cloth, oil, and honey. The men laughed at the gifts and said that gold was the only proper gift for the Zamorin. The Portuguese were allowed to sell their goods in Calicut, but the Muslim traders spread the word that the Portuguese products were cheaply made.

Da Gama had success trading with the Hindus and got samples of jewels and spices to bring home. When the sailors were ready to leave, the Zamorin refused to let

At his first meeting with the Zamorin of Calicut, shown here, da Gama said that he was hoping to find Christians who lived in the kingdom.

them go. He said da Gama needed to pay him a fee for being allowed to trade in Calicut. The two men worked out their disagreement, and the Zamorin sent a letter to King Manuel I saying that the Hindu ruler was pleased to have met da Gama.

VOYAGE HOME

During the long journey home, da Gama faced stormy weather and had to fight against many ships that tried to attack his fleet. The captain and his crew stopped in Malindi, where the friendly locals gave the Portuguese supplies. By then nearly one hundred crewmembers had died of scurvy. So many had passed away that da Gama didn't have enough men to sail his remaining three ships. He had already gotten rid of the store ship on the journey to India. Now he ordered his men to take supplies from the *São Rafael* and burn it.

The smaller fleet rounded the Cape of Good Hope in March 1499. Tragedy struck when Paulo da Gama became ill with tuberculosis. Paulo was too sick to make it

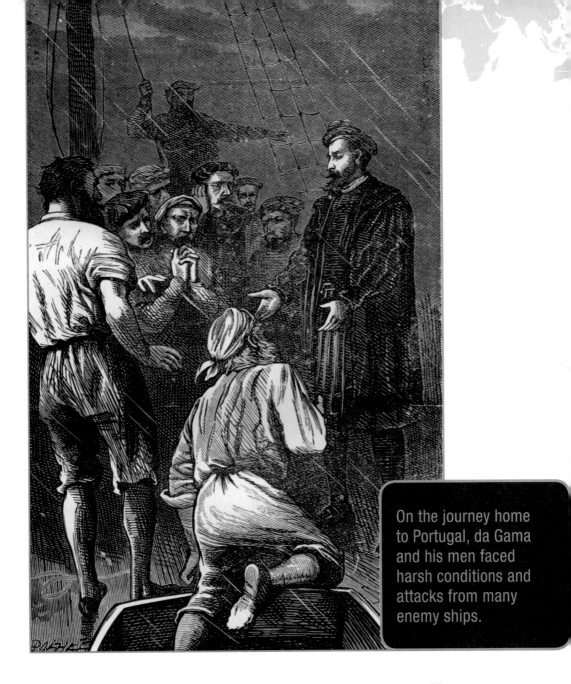

On the journey home to Portugal, da Gama and his men faced harsh conditions and attacks from many enemy ships.

home and died on the island of Teixeria, off the coast of Lisbon, in the summer of 1499. Da Gama was heartbroken over the death of his brother.

A CAUSE FOR CELEBRATION

Da Gama had sent the *São Gabriel* and the *Berrio* ahead to Lisbon while he stayed with his dying brother, Paulo. The arrival of those two ships was cause for much celebration. The crew had traveled over 24,000 miles (38,624 km) and been successful in the journey to India. This triumph was seen as equal to, if not greater than, Christopher Columbus's 1492 voyage to America. King Manuel I had warehouses built to store all the spices that would come to Portugal as a result of direct trade with India.

When da Gama returned, he was given the title of Dom, or Sir, to acknowledge his high position in society. He was also named

This picture depicts da Gama showing King Manuel I some of the treasures the Portuguese received on their journey to India.

Admiral of India and given the right to lead more expeditions. Da Gama collected a large yearly pension and was allowed to import spices from India without having to pay fees. Da Gama married Dona Catarina de Ataíde, the daughter of a high-ranking statesman, and started a family.

CABRAL'S JOURNEY TO INDIA

King Manuel I continued to send sea expeditions to India. In 1500, he sent Pedro Álvares Cabral to establish a trading base in Calicut. On the way to India, Cabral and his fleet of thirteen ships reached Brazil, along the eastern coast of South America. Cabral claimed Brazil as a colony for Portugal.

Once Cabral reached Calicut, events took a dark turn. There was a new Zamorin, and he and Cabral did not trust each other. In addition, the Muslim traders didn't want the Portuguese to establish a trading route to India because it would cut into their profits. The Portuguese seized a Muslim ship. In

retaliation, Muslim merchants attacked Portuguese men working in a newly built factory, killing more than fifty. Cabral attacked an entire Muslim fleet, killing or imprisoning hundreds of men.

After this bloody battle, Cabral had a better experience in Cochin, India, where he was able to get spices and other goods to bring home to Portugal.

DA GAMA'S SECOND VOYAGE

In February 1502, King Manuel I sent Admiral da Gama and a fleet of twenty ships back to India. King Manuel wanted to expand Portugal's trading interests. He also wanted to remove the Muslims from their positions of dominance in the spice trade and deal with the Zamorin of Calicut, who had been such a source of strife for Portugal.

By June most of the fleet rounded the Cape of Good Hope. In July the ships entered the port of the island of Kilwa, on Africa's east coast. Da Gama spoke to the ruler of Kilwa, a man named Amir Ibrahim, and insisted that his people agree to Portuguese rule. Da Gama also told Ibrahim

After landing by the island of Kilwa, shown here, da Gama insisted that its leader, a man named Amir Ibrahim, agree to Portuguese rule.

that he needed to give King Manuel a yearly gift of gold. If Ibrahim did not agree to these conditions, da Gama and his men would fire bombards at the capital city. Ibrahim had no choice but to agree.

THE MÎRÎ

Once in India, da Gama and his men encountered an Arab ship named the *Mîrî*. There were 240 men and fifty women and children on the ship. Most of these Muslims were returning from a pilgrimage to the holy city of Mecca. There were also a dozen of Calicut's wealthiest traders on the *Mîrî*. Da Gama captured the ship. One of the traders told da Gama that he could fill four ships in his Portuguese fleet with spices if he would set the passengers free. Da Gama refused and seized goods from the ship. He had all the weapons removed from the *Mîrî*.

On October 3, 1502, he ordered the ship burned to the ground, killing all of the people on board. Da Gama claimed that this vicious attack was to get back at the Muslims for

This illustration shows da Gama's attack on the *Mîrî*, a ship carrying nearly three hundred people, most of them Muslims returning from a pilgrimage to Mecca.

killing Portuguese men in Calicut. The burning of the *Mîrî* remains the most controversial part of da Gama's career as an explorer.

A STANDOFF IN CALICUT

After the burning of the *Mîrî*, da Gama spent a few months along India's coast. His goal was to make trade deals and to remove Muslim traders from positions of power. He visited the port cities of Cannanore, Cochin, and Calicut. In Calicut, the Zamorin told da Gama that he wanted a treaty with the Portuguese. Da Gama stated that there would be no peace until all Muslims were removed from the city. The Zamorin refused, saying that the Muslims in Calicut had always treated him fairly.

During this standoff, the Portuguese captured fishermen and raided their boats. This led the Zamorin to insist that the admiral

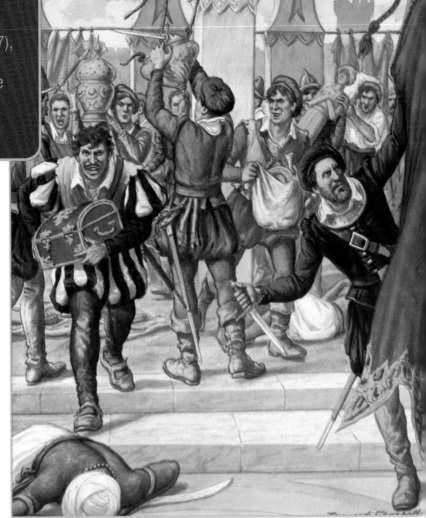

In this illustration by Italian artist Tancredi Scarpelli (1866–1937), the Portuguese are shown destroying the Zamorin of Calicut's royal palace.

give back everything he had taken from the *Mîrî*. An angry da Gama ordered that thirty-four men he had captured be hanged from the masts of his ships. Disgusted by this act, fighters from Calicut fired on the Portuguese but were soon overpowered. Much of Calicut was destroyed in the process.

A FIERCE BATTLE

In Cochin, da Gama met with the local ruler. The two men got along, even exchanging gifts. By 1502, Portugal had set up several factories in Cochin, so da Gama was able to load his ships with spices. While in the city, da Gama met with some leaders of a Christian group that had thirty thousand members. He was very happy to meet Indian Christians.

During his stay in Cochin, da Gama received a letter from the Zamorin. The Zamorin promised peace if da Gama would once again return to Calicut. In fact, the Zamorin had put together a fleet of seventy to eighty ships to attack the Portuguese.

During his second voyage to India, da Gama defeated the Zamorin, loaded his ships with spices like those shown here, and opened a factory in Cannanore.

There was a fierce battle, and a great many of the Zamorin's men lost their lives. Da Gama considered this success a great victory for his country. Before heading home to Portugal, da Gama set up a factory in the city of Cannanore.

YEARS AT HOME

U pon his return to Portugal in 1503, da Gama spent more than twenty years as a private citizen. During this time, he and his wife raised their family of seven children and moved back to da Gama's hometown of Sines. Da Gama wanted to be named lordship of Sines, but King Manuel I refused and told the admiral to leave the city. The king did agree to grant da Gama the title of Count.

While da Gama was home in Portugal, his country continued to expand its empire in South Asia. The Portuguese built colonies in places such as Cochin, Cannanore, and Goa in India. There were Portuguese viceroys in

A ILHA E CIDADE DE GOA METROPOLITANA DA INDIA E PARTES ORIENTAIS QVE ESTA EN 15 GRAOS DA BANDA DO NORTE.

This map from 1595 shows the island and city of Goa, India, which was a Portuguese colony for hundreds of years.

charge of these territories. King Manuel died in 1521, and John III, the new king, was worried that Portugal's interests were not being properly looked after. The king asked Count da Gama to go to India to serve as the new viceroy.

AN EXPLORER'S FINAL VOYAGE

Vasco da Gama began his final voyage to India in April 1524. Once there, he took on his duties as viceroy. He replaced officials who were considered unethical with men who were loyal to the king. In Goa, he issued an order stating that anyone who owned a ship had to sign a contract with the Portuguese or risk having his ship seized.

When he arrived in Cochin, da Gama worked tirelessly to make Portugal's empire more productive. By December 1524, he had become seriously ill. He made sure to choose his replacement as viceroy before dying on Christmas Eve.

For his forceful and at times cruel behavior, da Gama is a controversial figure in

DOM VASCO DA GAMA
1469-1524
DESCOBRIDOR E ALMIRANTE DO MAR DA IND
I° CONDE DA VIDIGUEIRA
VICE-REI DA INDIA

places such as Africa and India. In Portugal, however, he is largely viewed as a hero. His strengths as an explorer and a warrior helped make his small country a powerful force on the world stage.

GLOSSARY

bombard An early type of cannon that used stone balls to attack an enemy.

bubonic plague A bacterial illness that causes high fevers, vomiting, open sores, and extreme pain.

conch shell The shell of a sea snail, used as a musical instrument, as decoration, or as a form of money.

fleet A group of ships led by a single commander.

Malayalam The language of the Indian state of Kerala.

maritime Having to do with the sea.

Muslims People who follow the religion of Islam.

pension A fixed amount of money given on a regular basis; pensions can be given for various reasons, including past work, age, disability, or injury.

pilgrimage A journey to a sacred place that shows a person's commitment to a certain religion.

Portuguese Inquisition A court system set up by the Catholic Church that put people on trial for going against the teachings of the church.

scurvy A disease caused by a lack of vitamin C in the diet, causing weakness and problems with teeth, skin, and joints.

standoff A disagreement between two people or groups where neither side is willing to compromise.

strife Extreme conflict between two or more people.

tuberculosis An infectious disease spread from one person to another through the airborne droplets produced when coughing or sneezing.

unethical Without morals; acting in a dishonest way.

viceroy A person appointed to rule over a territory.

Houston Maritime Museum
2204 Dorrington
Houston, TX 77030
(713) 666-1910
Website: http://www.houstonmaritimemuseum.org
The Houston Maritime Museum provides information
   on the Age of Discovery, including voyages by
   Columbus, as well as later explorers.

Mariners' Museum and Park
100 Museum Drive
Newport News, VA 23606
(757) 596-2222
Website: http://marinersmuseum.org
The Mariners' Museum and Park has an Age of
   Exploration gallery that provides information about
   shipbuilding, navigation, and mapmaking.

Maritime Museum of British Columbia
634 Humboldt Street
Victoria, BC V8W 1A6
Canada
(250) 382-2869
Website: http://www.mmbc.bc.ca
The Maritime Museum of British Columbia has
   a collection of logbooks, personal papers,
   photographs, and other items that span from the
   eighteenth through the twentieth centuries. The
   museum also owns a fleet of three ships.

Metropolitan Museum of Art
1000 Fifth Avenue (at 82nd Street)
New York, NY 10028
(212) 535-7710
Website: http://www.metmuseum.org
The Metropolitan Museum of Art has a collection of
    original pieces of clothing worn during the Age
    of Discovery. There are also clocks and other
    scientific instruments from that time period on
    display.

Vancouver Maritime Museum
1905 Ogden Avenue in Vanier Park
Vancouver, BC V6J 1A3
Canada
(604) 257-8300
Website: http://www.vancouvermaritimemuseum.com
The Vancouver Maritime Museum offers an exhibit on
    the search for the Northwest Passage, a sea route
    connecting the Atlantic and Pacific oceans.

Websites

Because of the changing nature of Internet links,
Rosen Publishing has developed an online list of
websites related to the subject of this book. This site
is updated regularly. Please use this link to access
this list:

http://www.rosenlinks.com/SEC/gama

Bader, Bonnie. *Who Was Christopher Columbus?* New York, NY: Grosset & Dunlap, 2013.

Curley, Robert, ed. *Explorers of the Renaissance.* New York, NY: Britannica Educational Publishing, 2013.

DK Publishing. *Explorers: Tales of Endurance and Exploration.* New York, NY: DK Publishing, 2010.

Elliot, Lynne. *Exploration in the Renaissance.* New York, NY: Crabtree Publishing Company, 2009.

Krull, Kathleen. *Lives of the Explorers: Discoveries, Disasters (and What the Neighbors Thought).* New York, NY: Houghton Mifflin, 2014.

Matthews, Rupert. *Explorer.* New York, NY: DK Publishing, 2012.

Mooney, Carla. *Explorers of the New World.* Ann Arbor, MI: Nomad Press, 2011.

Napoli, Tony. *Vasco da Gama: Discovering the Sea Route to India.* New York, NY: Enslow Publishers, 2010.

Ross, Stewart. *Into the Unknown.* Somerville, MA: Candlewick Press, 2011.

BIBLIOGRAPHY

Ariganello, Lisa. *Henry the Navigator: Prince of Portuguese Exploration.* New York, NY: Crabtree Publishing Company, 2007.

Bailey, Katharine. *Vasco da Gama: Quest for the Spice Trade.* New York, NY: Crabtree Publishing Company, 2007.

Calvert, Patricia. *Vasco da Gama: So Strong a Spirit.* New York, NY: Marshall Cavendish, 2005.

Cliff, Nigel. *The Last Crusade.* New York, NY: HarperCollins, 2012.

Crowley, Roger. *Conquerors: How Portugal Forged the First Global Empire.* New York, NY: Random House, 2015.

Curley, Robert, ed. *Explorers of the Renaissance.* New York, NY: Britannica Educational Publishing, 2013.

Demi. *Columbus.* Las Vegas, NV: Amazon Publishing, 2012.

Gallagher, Jim. *Vasco da Gama and the Portuguese Explorers.* Warminster, PA: Chelsea House Publishers, 2000.

Rutsala, David. *The Sea Route to Asia.* Philadelphia, PA: Mason Crest Publishers, 2003.

Stefof, Rebecca. *Vasco da Gama and the Portuguese Explorers.* Warminster, PA: Chelsea House Publishers, 1993.

INDEX

About the Author

Jennifer Landau received her MA in creative writing from New York University and her MST in general and special education from Fordham University. An experienced editor, she has also published both fiction and nonfiction. She is an armchair traveler and history buff who loves learning about different cultures and time periods.

While researching this book, she was thrilled to discover that an unknown crewmember had kept a detailed logbook of da Gama's first voyage to India. *The Roteiro*, as it is known, proved fascinating reading. When she is not writing, Landau enjoys reading across all genres and spending time outdoors with her son.

Photo Credits